Forever
Paris

Forever
Paris

MONUMENTS, MUSEUMS, NEIGHBORHOODS, STREETS, SQUARES, PARKS AND GARDENS

Photographs Jacques Lebar

English adaptation by David W. Cox

PARIGRAMME

Paris forever... A city with such a wealth of urban promises might never exhaust them. Paris's miracle is the forever-renewed contemplation of its beauty; could anyone ever complain of having too often walked the banks of the Seine or of having overindulged in enjoying the symmetry of Place des Vosges?

Of course, the beauty of the city and our fascination with it are inseparable, but the reason for our enchantment cannot be reduced to a single facet. The Haussmann-period urban revival shaped the 19th-century face of an imperial capital but did not erase the noblest buildings, the grand city squares, or the 17th-century courts laid out by the construction kings, from Henri IV to Louis XIV. And the far older testimonies to the talent of architects in the Middle Ages continue to move passersby today. Closer to our own times, Art Déco, modern, and contemporary realizations contribute to a fabulous gallery of architecture.

This wealth, as one can guess, is not merely plastic. It is steeped and embedded in history which we can survey and savor at every street corner. History becomes tangible. Our hands can caress a sandy blond stone which countless other generations of hands have touched. In Paris, a permanent arrangement brings us the pleasures of sweeping panoramas, wide river vistas, plunging hilltop views over an ocean of zinc-slated rooftops. Our eyes pass from the delights of absorbing specific details to appreciating the overall harmony. The sense of unity doesn't result from any duplication of models but resides in a slow, centuries-old shaping of the streets.

This is history is also our own. It belongs to everyone who loves this city which sticks to the soles of our shoes. Our emotions, our recollections are spontaneously carved by and written into the cityscape. Our moods and its ambiances merge into a single climate. Bustling or cloistered, prestigious or working-class, traditional or exotic, multiple facets of Paris can be found within a one-block radius, taking us from one universe to one that's entirely different. Walking its avenues and passageways, we buzz from one ambiance to another, making our own honey. Isn't that quite simply the definition of bliss?

The Pont-Neuf is the oldest of Paris's bridges, inaugurated in 1607 by King Henri IV after thirty long years of construction. Innovating over other bridges of its time, it had no buildings lining its carriageways, thus turning it into a balcony offering a clear view of the Seine. Is this one of the reasons for its success? Parisians instantly liked it as it attracted all sorts of street performers.

Notre-Dame de Paris
is a great stone vessel
defying the laws of
navigation. Rooted
in the cityscape and
bathed by both the
stream of water and
the stream of time.

Before the cathedral's wide esplanade was laid out in the Second Empire, the only glimpse one could get of Notre-Dame's façade was at the last moment, turning a corner from out of one of the many narrow medieval streets, or, contrarily, from a great distance. Pilgrims and visitors in the Middle Ages would admire its silhouette and its towers rising over the rooftops. The gallery over the portals contains statues of the 28 kings of Judah, Christ's ancestors. In the Revolution, the statues were mistaken for monarchs of France and consequently were destroyed. The rose window in the south transept, modified in each century, depicts the celestial court arranged around the central figure of Christ and the four evangelists. Below it stand the sixteen prophets.

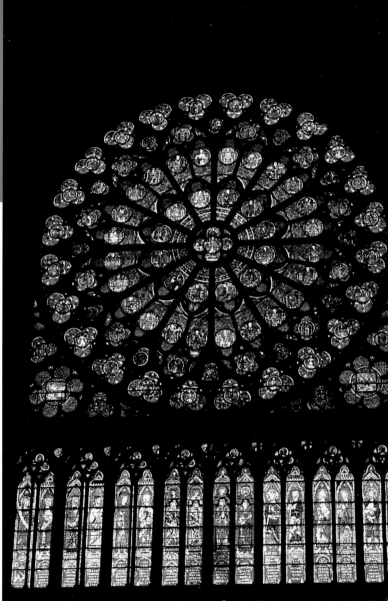

The west façade's rose window behind the statue of the Virgin escorted by two angels is the smallest in the cathedral. Recounting the life of Mary, its other themes include the labors of the months, virtues and vices, and prophets.

The central portal depicts the Last Judgment. Christ commands the Resurrection of the dead, expediting the good and the not-so-good to either heaven or hell. The 130-meter-long nave rises to a lofty 35 meters.

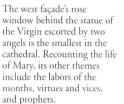

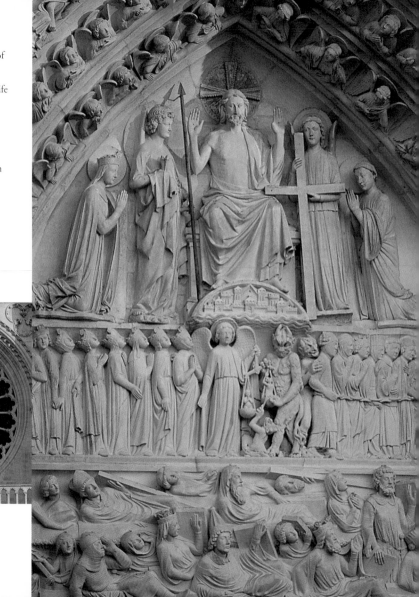

View from the Left Bank
of the apse with its flying
buttresses. The steeple
of Notre-Dame towers
90 meters over the city.

**Square René-Viviani-
Montebello.** This tiny garden
boasts an exceptional location
facing the cathedral. It also has
the privilege of being home to
the city's oldest tree, a Black
Locust, planted in 1601 and
now charitably propped by
a concrete crutch.

The Sainte-Chapelle.
The Sainte-Chapelle,
now hemmed in by the
Palais de Justice, was
built between 1246 and
1248 by Saint Louis
in a space that was then
inside the perimeter of
the royal palace. It was
intended to house relics
of the Passion: fragments
of Christ's crown of
thorns and pieces of the
cross.

The upper chapel, unlike the lower chapel intended for lower-ranking people in the palace, was reserved for the king and his entourage.

This architectural gem is famed for its precious relics (now integrated in the treasure of Notre-Dame), and its extraordinary stained-glass windows. Of the total 1,134 windows, over 700 are original.

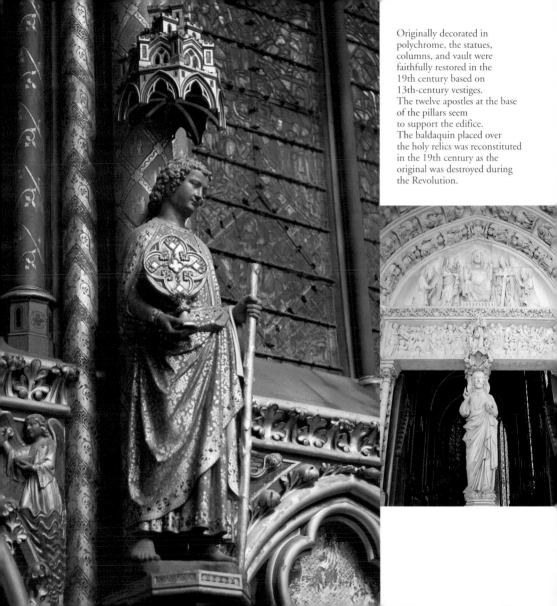

Originally decorated in
polychrome, the statues,
columns, and vault were
faithfully restored in the
19th century based on
13th-century vestiges.
The twelve apostles at the base
of the pillars seem
to support the edifice.
The baldaquin placed over
the holy relics was reconstituted
in the 19th century as the
original was destroyed during
the Revolution.

The Conciergerie. The four towers of the Conciergerie on Quai de l'Horloge, are remnants of much-renovated Palais Royal on Île de la Cité. The first, a square tower, is home to the city's oldest clock (1583). Next are the Tour César and the Tour d'Argent, and last, the Tour Bonbec, which in the Middle Ages got its nickname (candy tower) from the practice of torturing prisoners into talking.

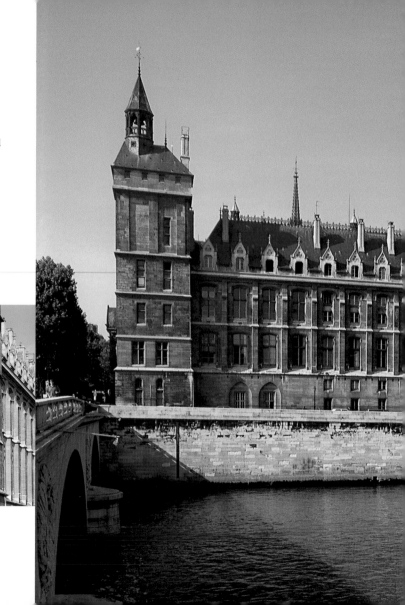

The Place Dauphine is the second oldest square in the city after Place Royale (now named Place des Vosges), laid out in the early 17th century by Henri IV, the urban design king.
Place Dauphine was named for the heir (dauphin) to the throne, the future Louis XIII.
Achille de Harlay, the first president of the parliament, oversaw the construction of 32 identical brick and stone homes along the three sides of a triangular green. One side is now missing. It was razed in 1874 to provide a clear view of the Palais de Justice which had to be monumental.
Only the two houses on the far end, beside Pont-Neuf, remain as originally planned.
The others have been altered and renovated. They face the equestrian statue of Henri IV, which, in 1818, replaced an older statue destroyed in the Revolution.

The Île Saint-Louis used to be two small islands in the Seine. In 1614, Christophe Marie, the city's bridge constructor, was commissioned by Louis XIII to fill in the arm of the river separating the two islands and to connect the new single island to the Right Bank with a bridge. That bridge bears its builder's name. An admirable 17th-century architectural ensemble. Rue Saint-Louis-en-l'Île runs straight through the island. A church bell tower (1765) rises high above the street.

The Île Saint-Louis is graced
by lovely homes and private
mansions. The most famous is
the Hôtel Lambert, designed
by Louis Le Vau, master of
classical architecture.
He built two other mansions
here before designing the
Vaux-le-Vicomte chateau, and
then, as first architect to the
king, extensions to Versailles.

A stroller's paradise,
the Île Saint-Louis also
offers relaxing sidewalk
cafés, restaurants, and the
famed Berthillon ice-cream
store.

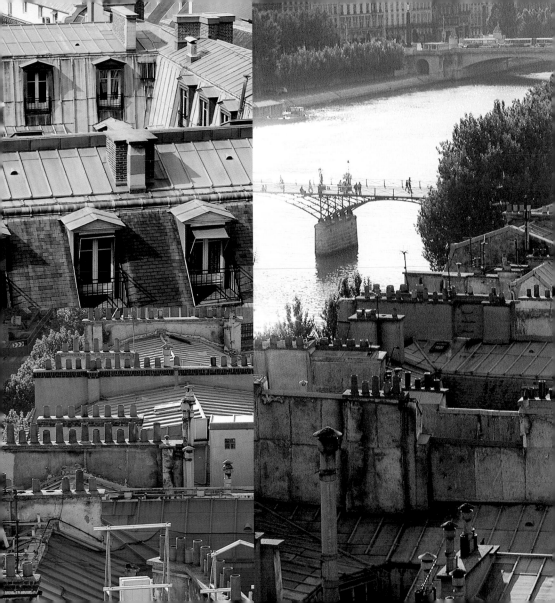

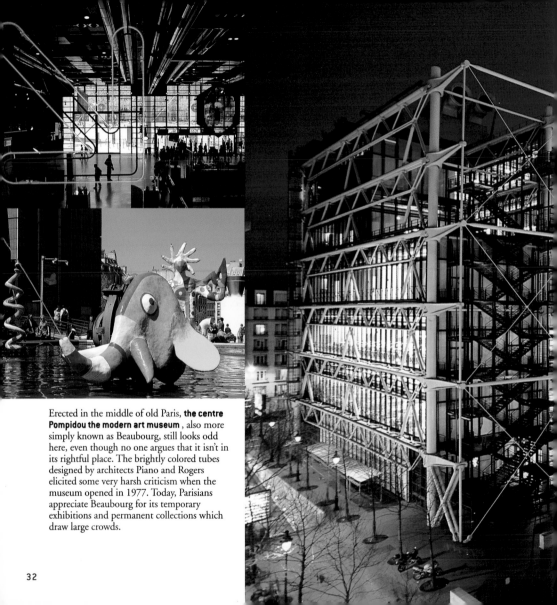

Erected in the middle of old Paris, **the centre Pompidou the modern art museum** , also more simply known as Beaubourg, still looks odd here, even though no one argues that it isn't in its rightful place. The brightly colored tubes designed by architects Piano and Rogers elicited some very harsh criticism when the museum opened in 1977. Today, Parisians appreciate Beaubourg for its temporary exhibitions and permanent collections which draw large crowds.

The Palais du Louvre.
The pyramid viewed from inside. It serves as the museum's main entrance and the emblem of the renovation of the "Grand Louvre", a program led by architect Ieoh Ming Pei from 1983 to 1996.

The grand colonnade along Rue de l'Amiral-de-Coligny was designed by Claude Perrault, the brother of Charles, known for his children's stories. It closed the Cour Carrée and gave the palace a majestic façade facing the city. But when Louis XIV abandoned the Louvre for Versailles, construction was suspended and only resumed under Louis XV.

Taking its cue from Roman antiquity, **the Arc du Carrousel** was erected under the Empire by Percier and Fontaine to celebrate Napoleon's military victories. It also marked the entrance to the now vanished Palais des Tuileries. The royal residence burned in 1871 during the Commune de Paris and was torn down afterwards.

In the Cour Napoléon, outside the pyramid, museum-goers form a long, meandering line.

The Louvre beneath the Louvre! Under the Cour Carrée, or more accurately under its southwestern quarter, are the foundations of the **medieval Louvre**, a veritable fortress erected under Philippe Auguste at the close of the 12th century. In the 16th century, King Francis I wanted to replace the old fortified castle with a Renaissance palace. He had the older structure razed but only to the ground so as to build upon the foundations. Today's visitors can enjoy exploring the medieval moat.

FOLLOWING PAGES:

Louvre Museum
Winged Victory of Samothrace (circa 190 B.C.)
Antonio Canova, *Psyche Revived by Cupid's Kiss* (1793)
Pierre Puget, *Perseus and Andromeda* (1664)
Assyrian Human Headed Winged Bull from Khorsabad (circa 720 B.C.)

The Carrousel and the Tuileries gardens make up a veritable open-air museum of sculpture. The Carrousel garden invites us to admire Aristide Maillol's famous bathing beauties, nymphs, and goddesses. They were placed here in 1964 on the orders of Minister of Culture André Malraux.

FOLLOWING PAGES:

The Tuileries garden is the oldest in Paris. The "Grand Carré" around the circular pool of water has changed little since it was designed by Le Nôtre in the 17th century.

The large octagonal pool in the Tuileries is a major feature of the central walkway as one heads toward Place de la Concorde. It mirrors the round pool at the opposite end of the Tuileries.

Outside the gates, along Rue de Rivoli, is **the Jeu de Paume**, a modern art museum housed in a Second Empire building. Major names in contemporary art are on display here.

The Place de la Concorde, the largest and most prestigious traffic square in Paris, was designed by Jacques Ange Gabriel, architect to Louis XV, as a westward extension of the city. During the Revolution, the guillotine that took the lives of Louis XVI, Marie-Antoinette, Robespierre, and many others was erected here.

The Place de la Concorde
was reorganized in the first
half of the 19th century
by the architect Hittorff
who set up the fountains,
the statues symbolizing
the nation's major cities,
and the ancient Egyptian
obelisk from Luxor.

The Grand Palais was erected for the 1900 Universal Exhibition. Its impressive 240-meter nave is capped by a splendid glass roof. While it may resemble delicate lacework, the metal structure weighs as much as the Eiffel Tower! Closed for many years due to structural deterioration, the Grand Palais finally reopened in 2007.

The Petit Palais, designed by Charles Girault, was also built for the 1900 Universal Exhibition as the hall celebrating France's artistic genius. Recently renovated, it now houses collections belonging to the city of Paris. The statue of Winston Churchill on the avenue is the work of Jean Cardot (1998).

The Avenue des Champs-Élysées looking toward Place de la Concorde.

FOLLOWING PAGES:

Avenue des Champs-Élysées, a majestic view of the Arc de Triomphe.

59

Napoleon wanted **the Arc de Triomphe** to celebrate his army's glorious victories, but it wasn't completed until 1836, long after the emperor's death. François Rude sculpted *La Marseillaise*, the impressive high relief pictured here. Beneath the arch lies the tomb of an unknown soldier who died in action in World War I. The Flamme du Souvenir (memorial flame) is lit every evening.

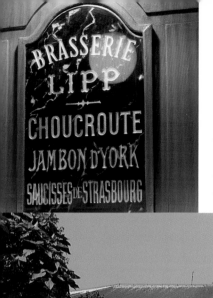

Paris is known for **fine food** of all sorts. Food lovers will dine with equal pleasure at Le Train Bleu (left), a splendid restaurant inside Gare de Lyon, at Ledoyen (below), a multiple-star address on the Champs-Élysées, or at Lipp, a Saint-Germain-des-Prés brasserie.

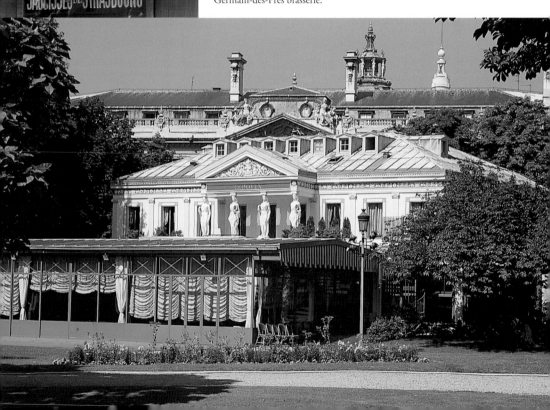

EUBLE PRIME
ICOURS DE FAÇADES
VILLE DE PARIS
UIMARD Architecte 1897-98

60

Paris's Art Nouveau movement had but a handful of representatives. **Hector Guimard** was one. His contemporaries weren't always very kind to him. One of his major works, the Castel Béranger located on Rue Fontaine in the 16th arrondissement, was jokingly called the "castel dérangé" (the deranged castle). Nevertheless, the architect designed several buildings and mansions, particularly in the 16th arrondissement. He also designed several of Paris's metro entrance structures such as this one at Porte Dauphine, still standing.

The Palais de Chaillot was built by Carlu, Boileau & Azéma for the 1937 Universal Exhibition. The architects very cleverly made use of the foundations of the old Palais du Trocadéro, which was built for the 1878 Exhibition.
It had two curved wings flanking the center portion designed as a rotunda with two minarets. The main thrust of the new project was to take the configuration of the curving wings, bring it in line wtih the taste of the 1930s, and replace the rotunda with an empty esplanade. What building could have possibly rivaled the nearby Eiffel Tower?
The Palais de Chaillot is home to the Théâtre National de Chaillot, the Musée de l'Homme, the Musée de la Marine, and since 2007 to the Cité de l'Architecture et du Patrimoine.

FOLLOWING PAGES:

The Fontaine de Varsovie
(Warsaw fountain)
located in the Trocadéro
gardens at the base of
the Palais de Chaillot.

The Bois de Boulogne was commissioned by Emperor Napoleon III for the pleasure of the high society, providing new leisurely strolls whether on foot, horseback or in horse-drawn carriages. Man-made lakes were poured, pathways were laid out, vegetation was planted, and park buildings were erected.

The Pavillon de Bagatelle antedates the park itself. In 1777, in a mere two months, it was built from top to bottom on the orders of the Count of Artois, Louis XVI's brother, to win the bet he had made with his sister-in-law, Marie-Antoinette. The property was reorganized by the Marquess of Hertford in the 19th century, then by his son, Sir Richard Wallace, who had his own Trianon built here.

The Parc Monceau, a landscaped ornamental garden, is the distant heir to the Orléans family's estate that was carved up in Second Empire real estate deals. The park underwent extensive renovation to meet the needs of the times. A few original elements remain, however, for example, the famous naumachia. The colonnade was probably dismantled from the Valois chapel in the Saint-Denis abbey. The rotunda near the park entrance is one of the last standing pavilions designed by Ledoux for the Fermiers Généraux city wall.

The Paris Opera, the height of the florid Napoleon III style known for its abundance of color, gilding, and sculptures, was designed by Charles Garnier and inaugurated in 1875. The grand staircase was designed for the pomp of imperial gatherings.

PREVIOUS PAGES:

Place de l'Opéra.

METRO

M 7 9 Chaussée d'Antin
La Fayette

Department stores turn on the magic for the holiday season, making **the Boulevard Haussmann** a river of light.

The Place Vendôme, designed during the reign of Louis XIV, is a showcase for some of Paris's top jewelers. The column in the center stands 44 meters high. It was erected by Napoleon I to celebrate the victory at Austerlitz.

What began as the Palais-Cardinal, built by and for Cardinal Richelieu, was bequeathed to the crown of France and became **the Palais-Royal**. It was rebuilt after the 1763 fire. From 1781 to 1784, the Duke of Orleans divided the property into lots; those bordering the gardens became rental properties and ground-floor shops. As a princely domain off limits to the police, the Palais-Royal quickly became a mecca for gamblers and ladies of the night. It was also a gathering place for rabble-rousing revolutionaries.

Today's Palais-Royal is known for its calm. It is home to the Ministry of Culture, the Conseil d'État (Council of State) and other residents of equally respectable behavior. The main courtyard features Pol Bury's spherical sculptures and Daniel Buren's black and white columns.

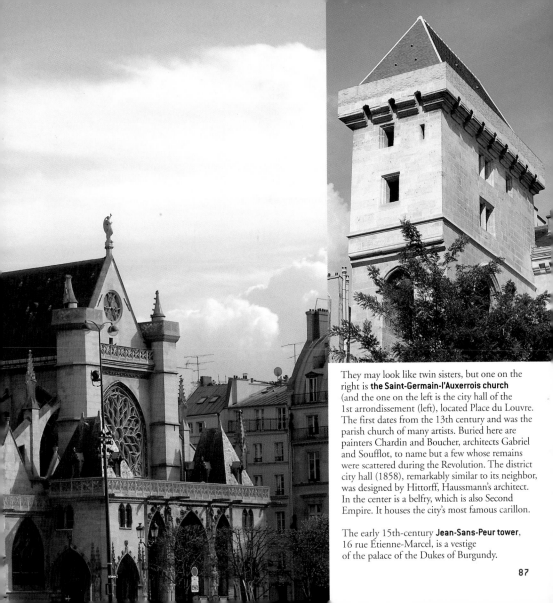

They may look like twin sisters, but one on the right is **the Saint-Germain-l'Auxerrois church** (and the one on the left is the city hall of the 1st arrondissement (left), located Place du Louvre. The first dates from the 13th century and was the parish church of many artists. Buried here are painters Chardin and Boucher, architects Gabriel and Soufflot, to name but a few whose remains were scattered during the Revolution. The district city hall (1858), remarkably similar to its neighbor, was designed by Hittorff, Haussmann's architect. In the center is a belfry, which is also Second Empire. It houses the city's most famous carillon.

The early 15th-century **Jean-Sans-Peur tower**, 16 rue Étienne-Marcel, is a vestige of the palace of the Dukes of Burgundy.

87

In 1969, **Les Halles**, then Paris's main food market, moved out of the center of the capital to the suburb of Rungis. A shopping mall was built to fill the void, but the new architecture never received much enthusiasm. The Forum des Halles is currently undergoing a thorough renovation by several architectural firms. Today, Les Halles' claim to fame is as the world's largest underground subway station. Three RER (regional express) lines cross in this city-center transport hub, making it the station most frequented by Île-de-France inhabitants.

The astrological column erected in 1578 is all that is left of the residence of the superstitious Catherine de Médicis. The queen's home was located on the present-day site of the Bourse du Commerce, which, prior to that, housed a grain market.

It took nearly ninety years to build **Saint-Eustache church** (1532-1640). The reason it took so long was the difficulty in mixing Gothic forms with Renaissance decoration. It was the parish church of Les Halles merchants and laborers, yet it was here that Richelieu, Madame de Pompadour, and Molière were baptized. Colbert is buried in the church.

The bustling **Rue Montorgueil**, still full of shops and cafés today, once marked the end of the journey for carts laden with seafood and fish from northern harbors like Calais and Boulogne.

Les Halles has long been known for its fine restaurants such as **L'Escargot Montorgueil** with its unchanged interior décor and its exterior wood paneling, and the **Pied de Cochon** on Rue Coquillière, open 24 hours a day, whose doors have never once been closed for business since the day it opened in 1946!

Laid out in the first half of the 19th century, Paris's covered passageways were shopping galleries allowing customers the pleasure of window shopping protected from the elements in a luxurious and well-lit setting.

The Galerie Véro-Dodat (left), created in 1826, was the brainchild of two delicatessen owners who became wealthy during the Restoration of the Bourbons (1830). Above, **the Passage Jouffroy** (below) was probably the last of the 19th-century Parisian shopping galleries (1846).

93

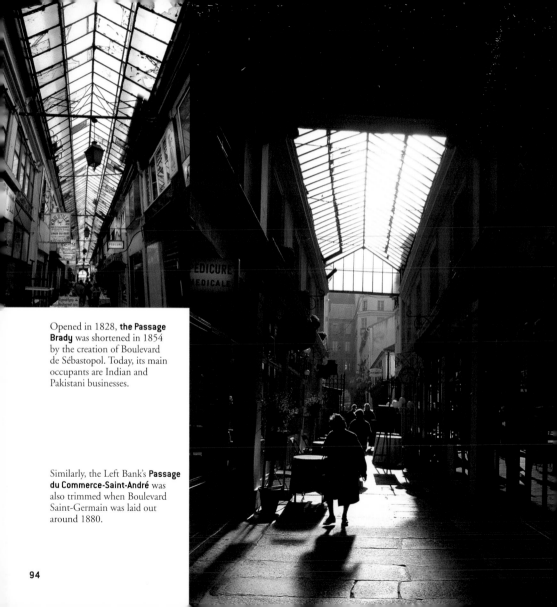

Opened in 1828, **the Passage Brady** was shortened in 1854 by the creation of Boulevard de Sébastopol. Today, its main occupants are Indian and Pakistani businesses.

Similarly, the Left Bank's **Passage du Commerce-Saint-André** was also trimmed when Boulevard Saint-Germain was laid out around 1880.

The Galerie Vivienne is the most elegant of the capital's shopping galleries. It connects the Palais-Royal neighborhood with the Bourse and the boulevards. It was an instant hit upon its inauguration in 1826.

The Passage des Panoramas was opened in 1799 and was expanded with other galleries in 1834.

The Passage du Caire
(1798) is one of the city's oldest existing passageways. It is also the longest as its three galleries total 370 meters. Most of its occupants are cloth wholesalers.

In 1860, Haussmann signed the order to create **the Passage des Princes** (right). It was the last of the 19th-century covered passageways. It was razed and rebuilt in 1995 in a neighborhood renovation project.

FOLLOWING PAGES:
The roofs of **Paris city hall**, and, in the background, **the Sacré-Cœur basilica** in Montmartre.

The Marais is a miraculously preserved enclave of 17th-century architecture. It has the city's highest concentration of mansions.

The Hôtel Carnavalet, located on Rue de Sévigné, is home to the museum of Paris history.

The Hôtel de Soubise, located on Rue des Francs-Bourgeois, has a vast main courtyard which underscores the majesty of the building and the prestige of its early 18th-century owner, François Rohan, prince de Soubise. The mansion has been home to the National Archives for two centuries.

Corbelled square turret, The Hôtel de Lamoignon at the corner of Rue des Francs-Bourgeois and Rue Pavée.

Grotesque figure, Rue Saint-Martin.

The Hôtel de Lamoignon, on Rue Pavée,
was built in 1611 for Diane de France,
illegitimate daughter of Henri II.
It acquired its name when it passed
into the hands of the Lamoignon
family, known for its lawyers and
members of parliament in the days
of the monarchy. Today, it is home to
the Bibliothèque Historique de la Ville
de Paris (the history of Paris library).

The Hôtel Salé. Garden-side façade viewed from Rue Vieille-du-Temple, now the home of the Picasso Museum. This mansion was built in the mid-17th century for Aubert de Fontenay, a man who grew rich collecting the salt tax, which explains the name of his residence (*salé*=salty).

Staircase, **Hôtel de Bonneval**, on Rue du Parc-Royal, painted in the Romantic period, first half of the 19th century.

A high-relief representing the Sun's horses over the stable door at **the Hôtel de Rohan**, Rue Vieille-du-Temple.

Medusa with serpents in her hair decorating a corner of the garden-side wing of **the Hôtel d'Hozier**, Rue Vieille-du-Temple.

The Hôtel de Donon, on Rue Elzévir, erected in the last quarter of the 16th century for Médéric de Donon, the king's general building inspector. The building now houses collections from the Cognacq-Jay Museum.

The Hôtel de Sens, rue du Figuier, built between the end of the 15th and the early 16th centuries by Tristan de Salazar, bishop of Sens. It and the Hôtel de Cluny are the city's oldest mansions. Turbulent Queen Margot took up residence at the Hôtel de Sens after her marriage

The Place des Vosges came to be following a decision by Henri IV to endow Paris with a silk factory, which was to have its own square for festivities and be surrounded by houses for artisans. The factory was short-lived and the workshops were torn down in 1607, less than two years after their construction. They were replaced by a row of buildings designed to match the other rows facing the square.

Simply called "*la place*" in the 16th century, Place des Vosges is lined, on each side, by nine brick and stone buildings (or materials imitating brick). The ground floors are recessed to accommodate arcaded galleries to protect passersby from inclement weather.

The Bastille has been a point of reference in French history since July 14, 1789. The demolition of the fortress-prison marks the start of the Revolution. Today, it is reduced to a mere outline on the paving stones of the traffic circle. But another equally massive building now stands on the other side of Place de la Bastille.

The Opéra Bastille was inaugurated on July 14, 1989 for the bicentennial. Rue de Lappe and the surrounding area known as the Faubourg Saint-Antoine are chock full of trendy sidewalk cafés, bars, restaurants.

The Faubourg Saint-Antoine used to be Paris's furniture-making center. Today, the area has but a handful of workshops. Most of the furniture-making courtyards of yesteryear have been renovated as homes and offices. This district kindled most of the movements that sparked reform in the 18th and 19th centuries.

The façade of the legendary hotel overlooking **the Canal Saint-Martin** still has its *atmosphère*, to quote the famous dialogue delivered by actress Arletty in Marcel Carné's masterpiece *Hôtel du Nord*. The canal's wharves used to be lined with warehouses and workshops. Today, they sport a new generation of chic cafés, shops, and restaurants.

At the top of the Butte
Montmartre, **the Sacré-Cœur**
stands out in the Paris skyline.
It was built over a forty-year
period to atone for losses in
the Franco-Prussian war and
the woes caused by the
Commune of 1871. It is a
pilgrimage and a sanctuary
of the perpetual adoration,
a round-the-clock prayer,
which has been constantly
relayed since the basilica's
consecration in 1916.

The Sacré-Cœur basilica and its gardens sloping steeply to Place Saint-Pierre.

The butte's leg-killer stairs figure in many popular songs.

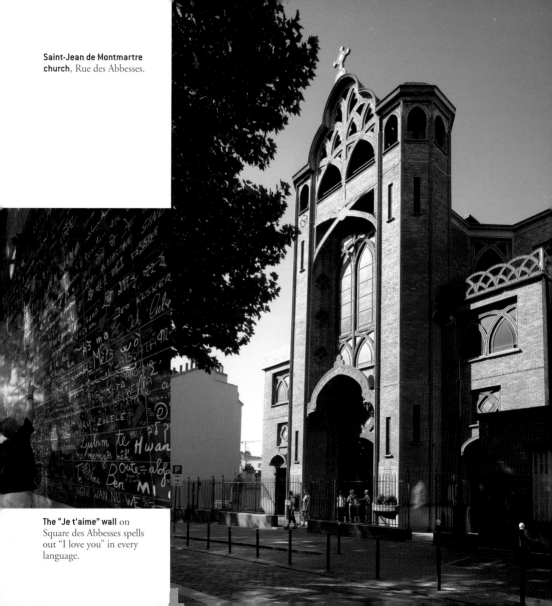

Saint-Jean de Montmartre church, Rue des Abbesses.

The "Je t'aime" wall on Square des Abbesses spells out "I love you" in every language.

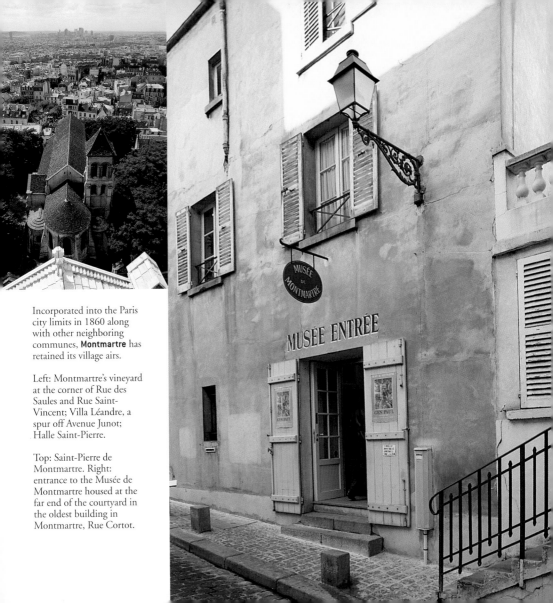

Incorporated into the Paris city limits in 1860 along with other neighboring communes, **Montmartre** has retained its village airs.

Left: Montmartre's vineyard at the corner of Rue des Saules and Rue Saint-Vincent; Villa Léandre, a spur off Avenue Junot; Halle Saint-Pierre.

Top: Saint-Pierre de Montmartre. Right: entrance to the Musée de Montmartre housed at the far end of the courtyard in the oldest building in Montmartre, Rue Cortot.

Le Lapin Agile, a famous cabaret on Rue des Saules, frequented by Renoir, Picasso, Utrillo, Van Gogh, and many other famous artists. It got its name from a sign painted by André Gill featuring a rabbit (*lapin* in French) dancing in a skillet. The name *Le Lapin à Gill* (Gill's rabbit) was quickly turned into *Le Lapin Agile* (the agile rabbit).

Place du Tertre is lined with homes that have barely changed since the 18th century.

Left: 6 Rue Norvins: the restaurant La Mère Catherine.

Left: The Blute-Fin, one of the two surviving **Montmartre windmills** stands on a private street. It can best be seen from 75 Rue Lepic. It and its neighboring sister windmill, Le Radet, hosted the ball known as le bal du moulin de la Galette featured in Renoir's famous painting of the same name.

Right: Moulin Radet at the corner of Rue Lepic and Rue Girardon.

Above : **Villa des Arts**, Rue Hégésippe-Moreau.

Right: **Place des Abbesses**.

The Parc des Buttes-Chaumont
was created by Alphand, the
engineer and landscapist, during
Haussmann's urban renewal
programs. The steeply sloping site
stood atop abandoned gypsum
quarries. Man-made cliffs and old
tunnel entrances were integrated
into the landscape design.
Tons of fertile earth were hauled
in to build up the thin topsoil.

The Parc de la Villette was laid out on the vast site freed when the Paris slaughterhouses went bankrupt in 1974. La Grande Halle, built in 1867, still stands and is used for shows and festivals.

The Cité des Sciences et de l'Industrie (the children's science museum) moved into the shell of the old Villette slaughterhouses and meat market. The floor space is roughly equivalent to the size of Place de la Concorde. The park grounds are populated by quirky red objects dreamed up by architect Bernard Tschumi, the Géode, a hemispherical Imax cinema contained in a polished steel sphere with a 36-meter diameter, the Cité de la Musique, both conservatory and museum, designed by Christian de Portzamparc, and the Zénith, a huge concert hall.

The 20th century brought an explosion of **architectural innovation** to the Paris cityscape and fresh ideas in renovating older structures.

Left: Le Centquatre, at 104 Rue d'Aubervilliers (19th), once the city morgue, now as a multipurpose cultural center. Below: La Cité de la Mode now housed in the old Magasins Généraux on Quai d'Austerlitz (13th), and the Ministry of Culture on Rue Saint-Honoré (1st).
Top: The Flower-Tower, Rue Albert-Roussel (17th) and the Université Paris-Diderot, in the former flour mills (Grands Moulins de Paris), on Quai Panhard et Levassor (13th).
Right: La Cité de l'Architecture et du Patrimoine, in the Palais de Chaillot, Place du Trocadéro (16th), took over the site formerly occupied by the Musée des Monuments Français.

Sprawling 44 hectares (108 acres), **Père Lachaise cemetery** is Paris's largest. It was laid out in the early 19th century on a hill then outside the city limits. The cemetery is famous as the final resting place of celebrities such as Frédéric Chopin, Édith Piaf, Oscar Wilde, Jim Morrison, Nancy Cunard, and Michel Petrucciani.

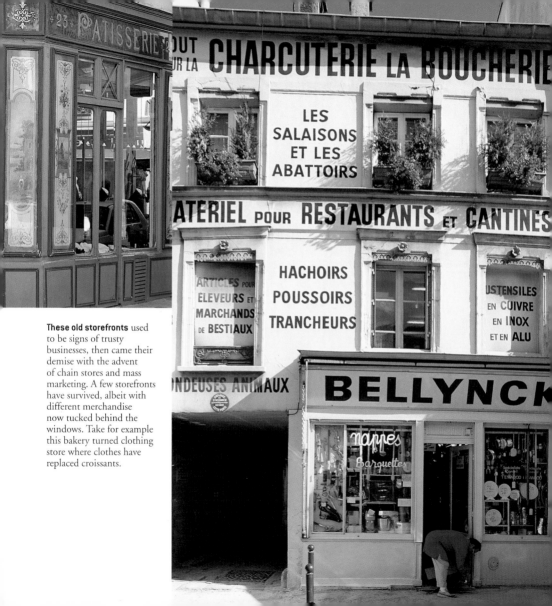

These old storefronts used to be signs of trusty businesses, then came their demise with the advent of chain stores and mass marketing. A few storefronts have survived, albeit with different merchandise now tucked behind the windows. Take for example this bakery turned clothing store where clothes have replaced croissants.

Narrow passageways with provincial ambiances – some private, some public – enchant amateurs of urban poetry.

Passage d'Enfer (14th), near Montparnasse. The name comes from the wood that used to cover this quarter.

Cité des Fleurs (17th) forking off of Avenue de Clichy.

Opposite: **Rue Berton** (16th), back entrance to Balzac's home. The novelist used it to avoid his numerous debt collectors.

In the nooks and crannies of the capital, one can still find the charm of **old village houses**, country subdivisions, extravagant follies, artists' studios, etc. Bliss just around the street corner?

Top: Rue Santos-Dumont (15th); Left: Cité de Varenne (7th) and Square Vergennes (15th).

Above: La Campagne
à Paris (20th) and
Hameau Boileau (16th).

Right: Saint-Germain-
de-Charonne (20th)
and La Ruche, Passage
de Dantzig (15th), which
still accommodates many
artists.

Bicycling is the best way to discover Paris, and it can also be the fastest and most ecological way to get around the city (faster than on four wheels). Since July 2007, over 20,000 Vélib' rental bikes and nearly 1,500 Vélib' bike stations have taken over the streets of the capital. In 2009, the automated bicycle rental service began branching out to nearby suburbs.

Paris Bridges

The oldest bridge in the capital is the Pont Neuf. Built in 1607 with no houses bordering its carriageway, it was the city's first to offer users a panorama of the Seine. Today, no less than 37 bridges span the river, giving pedestrians as many points of view, and recounting innumerable facets of the city's history.

Left: the Pont des Arts between the Louvre and the Institut de France; above: the Pont Charles-de-Gaulle, then the Viaduc and Pont d'Austerlitz.

159

Left: The graceful curves of Passerelle Simone de Beauvoir, between the Bibliothèque François Mitterrand and the Jardins de Bercy. Below: Passerelle Debilly by the Musée d'Art Moderne and Pont Alexandre III.

Opposite: Pont au Double, Petit-Pont and Pont Saint-Michel, between the Left Bank and Île de la Cité.

A smaller-scale copy of the Statue of Liberty proudly placed in front of Pont de Grenelle.

Pont des Arts in front of Pont-Neuf.

Quais of the Seine: near
Pont de Bir-Hakeim.

FOLLOWING PAGES:

The Pont Alexandre III
was named for Russia's czar
who laid the bridge's first
stone. It was inaugurated
in 1900 for the Universal
Exhibition. The bridge not
only takes traffic to Avenue
Winston Churchill, the
Grand Palais and the Petit
Palais, it offers splendid
views of Les Invalides.

In an odd quirk of fate, **the Eiffel Tower** became the symbol of Paris for the entire world although it was severely criticized by the most influential writers and artists of the time, who demanded it be dismantled. Gustave Eiffel erected what was then the world's highest monument for the 1889 Universal Exhibition. A 300-meter-high tower could never have been designed had it not been for recent developments in metal architectural structures.

Assembled from prefabricated elements manufactured in Eiffel's workshops (which also produced the Statue of Liberty for New York City's harbor), the tower was completed in two years. After the Universal Exhibition, a reason had to be found to keep it from being torn down. Providential progress provided that reason in the form of antennas for radio (then later, television) broadcasting which needed the highest possible perches. But it was the general public's enthusiasm which turned the Tower into Europe's most popular monument, thus giving it a new lease on life.

The Quai Branly Museum opened in 2006. The building designed by Jean Nouvel houses art and artifact collections from all five continents. Skewering the main building is a long ramp leading to various siderooms filled with collections and represented on the façades by colored boxes. The administrative building's quay-side façade dripping with vegetation is a green wall designed by Patrick Blanc.

If you think **the Musée d'Orsay** has a train station aura about it, you're right. It used to be one. It belonged to the Paris-Orléans train company providing train service between these two cities. Orsay was designed to be the more prestigious and centrally-located extension of the out-of-the-way Gare d'Austerlitz for passengers arriving from Bordeaux, Saintes, Toulouse, and Poitiers. It turned out to be impractical and, although inaugurated in 1900, it closed in the late 1930s. After a long period of indecision, Victor Laloux's Belle Époque building was given a new job: to house Paris's new museum devoted to 19th-century art. Opened in 1986, the Musée d'Orsay's remarkable collections include paintings by the masters of Impressionism.

175

The Hôtel des Invalides was set up by Louis XIV for soldiers wounded in military campaigns. The statue of Napoleon placed in the main courtyard came from the Vendôme Column, on which it stood from 1833 to 1863.

The Invalides' gilded domed church was designed by Jules Hardouin-Mansart. Erected beside the more austere soldiers' church, the contrast is heightened by its distinctly royal entrance, which would have been further underscored by a colonnade delimiting the impressive main courtyard. The church is capped by the highest and finest 17th-century domes in all of Paris. Beneath this dome are the tombs of great soldiers, and in the center of the crypt is the tomb of Napoleon I.

Parmentier, the Invalides' pharmacist, is known to have used the superintendent's garden to test a promising new tuber called the potato.

Quiet courtyard off Rue du Cherche-Midi.

The Saint-Germain-des-Prés abbatial palace (above) was built in 1586 for the uncle of Henri IV, Cardinal Charles de Bourbon. It was one of the first brick and stone constructions in Paris, a style that would be repeated on Place des Vosges and Place Dauphine.

Beneath the bell tower of **Saint-Germain-des-Prés**, the only tower in Paris to have traversed a thousand years of often agitated history, are tranquil courtyards, art galleries and antique shops.

Left: The corner sidewalk café Le Bar du Marché in the bustling market area of Rue de Buci and Rue de Seine is a fine spot for watching the world go by.

A tangle of windows, chimneys, conduits, and skylights at the intersection of Rue Bourbon-le-Château and Rue de l'Échaudé.

185

Dolce vita Paris-style,
Place de l'Odéon,
on the esplanade
in front of the Théâtre
de l'Odéon.

The Luxembourg palace
was designed by Salomon
de Brosse for Marie de
Médicis when the queen
wanted to leave the
Louvre after her husband
Henri IV was assassinated
in 1610. At her request,
the architects borrowed
heavily from the design
of the Palazzo Pitti in
Florence. Marie de
Médicis only resided here
for five years before being
banished to Compiègne,
then forced into exile.
The palace now houses
the Senate and its offices.

The loveliest garden on the Left Bank is **the Luxembourg**. Parisians of all ages and tourists from all corners flock here to relax, revel, and stroll.
The area beside the large pool with its group of white statues of queens of France is a favorite for sun worshippers.

Everyday sights at Luxembourg Gardens: meditative chess players, bees buzzing in and out of their hive, Polyphemus the Cyclops at the Médicis fountain readying to hurl a bolder at Acis and Galatea.

A short walk from the Luxembourg palace is **the Pantheon**. Since the Revolution, the Pantheon has been a veritable temple to the greats of this world. It is the final resting place of Voltaire, Jean-Jacques Rousseau, Victor Hugo, Émile Zola, Jean Jaurès, Jean Moulin, Pierre and Marie Curie. It wasn't originally designed to be a non-religious, republican necropolis. Louis XV commissioned the architect Soufflot to erect a church dedicated to Saint Geneviève. Work wasn't completed until 1790, twenty-five years after the first stone had been laid. The church was turned into a mausoleum as early as 1791, then twice returned to being a place of worship during the Empire and the Second Empire, and finally, in 1873, resumed its current function.

The dome of the Panthéon rises high over **the Latin Quarter**. Further in the distance, are the bell tower of Saint-Étienne-du-Mont and the old Clovis tower ensconced in Lycée Henri IV. In the foreground, the courtyard of Lycée Louis-le-Grand.

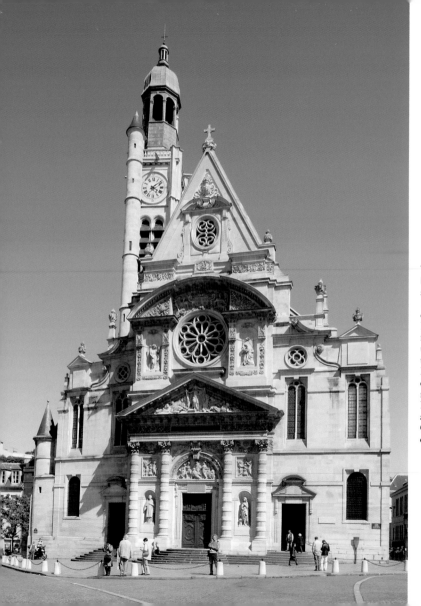

The construction of **Saint-Étienne-du-Mont church** spanned the years 1492-1626. As a result, it is a mix of Gothic, Renaissance, and Baroque styles. It is famous for its stunning rood screen, unique in Paris. It crosses the entire width of the nave. Furthermore, Saint-Étienne-du-Mont contains the reliquary of Saint Geneviève. Her remains were removed and burned on Place de Grève during the mad days of the Revolution.

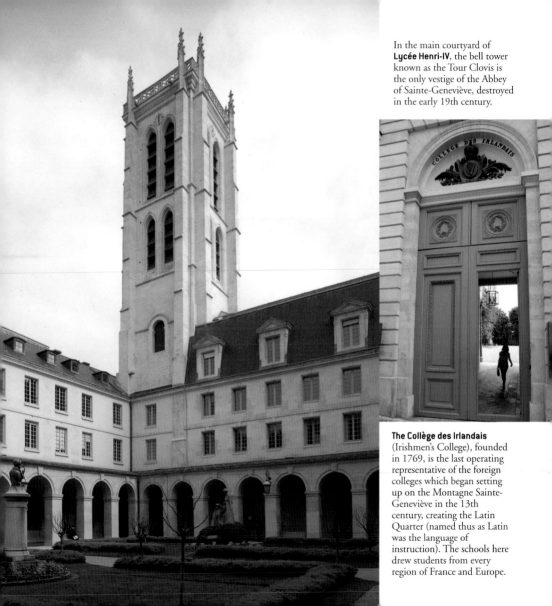

In the main courtyard of **Lycée Henri-IV**, the bell tower known as the Tour Clovis is the only vestige of the Abbey of Sainte-Geneviève, destroyed in the early 19th century.

The Collège des Irlandais (Irishmen's College), founded in 1769, is the last operating representative of the foreign colleges which began setting up on the Montagne Sainte-Geneviève in the 13th century, creating the Latin Quarter (named thus as Latin was the language of instruction). The schools here drew students from every region of France and Europe.

The Lycée Louis-le-Grand, the descendant of Collège de Clermont, the most prestigious of the Latin Quarter colleges is still the model for the city's most select high schools.

The monumental Fontaine Saint-Michel was erected by Davioud in the Second Empire as part of Haussmann's program for Boulevard Saint-Michel. It has long been a Latin Quarter meeting place.

The Place de la Sorbonne with its attractive cafés is generally more animated than the university's interior courtyard. As the city's first university, the Sorbonne is also a symbol. In 1250, Robert de Sorbon founded his college in the Latin Quarter. Richelieu ordered a complete renovation of the old building and commissioned architect Lemercier to build a new chapel which is the only vestige of Richelieu's 17th-century college. The school was entirely rebuilt in the late 19th century.

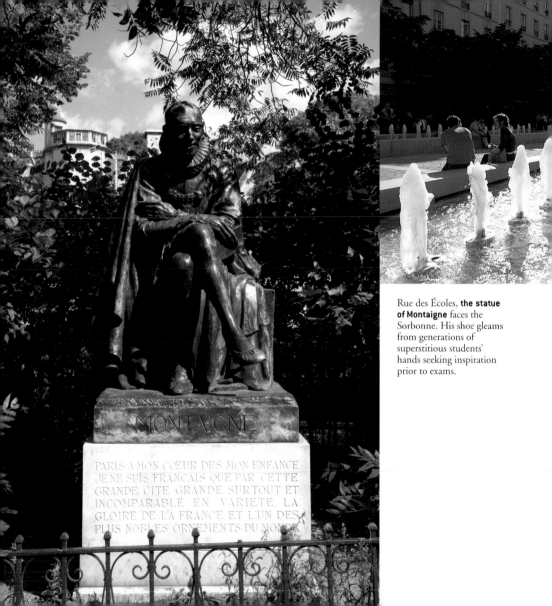

Rue des Écoles, **the statue of Montaigne** faces the Sorbonne. His shoe gleams from generations of superstitious students' hands seeking inspiration prior to exams.

MONTAIGNE

PARIS A MON CŒUR DES MON ENFANCE
JE NE SUIS FRANÇAIS QUE PAR CETTE
GRANDE CITÉ GRANDE SURTOUT ET
INCOMPARABLE EN VARIÉTÉ. LA
GLOIRE DE LA FRANCE ET L'UN DES
PLUS NOBLES ORNEMENTS DU MONDE

The English-language bookshop Shakespeare & Company on Rue de la Bûcherie was founded in 1951 by the grandson of American poet Walt Whitman. It took its name from the legendary bookshop run by Sylvia Beach from 1921 to 1941 on Rue de l'Odéon.

Lunch break, **Rue Descartes**.

On the corner of **Rue Mouffetard**, a Left-Bank market street.

The Art Deco **Pontoise swimming pool** in Latin Quarter.

Perched on its promontory, the restaurant Chez Léna et Mimile overlooks quaint **Place Lucien Herr**.

Rue Tournefort. Time seems to have stopped here. The old house at number 30 may have been the inspiration for Madame Vauquer's boarding house in Balzac's novel *Le Père Goriot*.

The second-century Roman **amphitheater (arena) of Lutetia** is actually older than the Cluny baths. The amphitheater could seat 17,000 spectators. This rare vestige of the Roman period had completely vanished from the cityscape until it was rediscovered when Rue Monge was created in the late 19th century. Without the active lobbying of Victor Hugo and other intellectuals, the Roman amphitheater would have been razed. The renovation wasn't completed until 1917.

Founded in the 13th century, for over four centuries **the Collège des Bernardins** was the leading center of intellectual events. In the Revolution, it became national property and was turned first into a warehouse, then a fire station, and finally a police school.
The building was only recently restored. It has become a conference and research center under the aegis of the Paris diocese.

The world-famous **Tour d'Argent** offers an exceptional view of Paris, the Seine and the apse of Notre-Dame. The early history of the restaurant is a tangled web of history and legend going back to its founding days under Henri III in the 16th century. We do know the establishment gained its world-class rank by serving crowned princes, theater stars, and business magnates. It has served hundreds of thousands of plates of its famed specialty, duck in blood sauce.

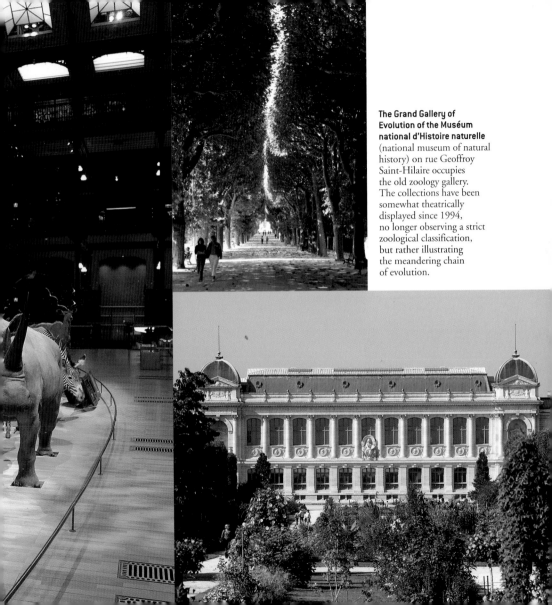

The Grand Gallery of Evolution of the Muséum national d'Histoire naturelle (national museum of natural history) on rue Geoffroy Saint-Hilaire occupies the old zoology gallery. The collections have been somewhat theatrically displayed since 1994, no longer observing a strict zoological classification, but rather illustrating the meandering chain of evolution.

The Bibliothèque nationale de France François Mitterrand is France's new location for its national library. Its four skyscrapers have altered the 13th arrondissement's skyline and brought renewal to its riverside neighborhoods. There are new leisure activities, too, such as the Batofar, a decommissioned boat turned bar and concert hall which attracts large crowds.

The capital is graced by no fewer than 400 **gardens and green spaces**. Some used to belong to private estates, others stand on former industrial sites, while smaller squares offer a respite of greenery in a concrete jungle.

Above: Parc André Citroën (15th).

Above and opposite: Parc Georges Brassens (15th).

Right: Musée Rodin garden.
The Thinker by Auguste Rodin (7th);
Parc de Belleville (20th) offering
a sweeping view of the cityscape.

Parc Floral and Arboretum
in the Bois de Vincennes
(12th).

Kiosque de l'Empereur
in the Bois de Boulogne
(16th).

Square du Vert-Galant
(Île de la Cité, 1st).

Square Louvois (2nd).

Bust of Dora Maar by Picasso, Square Laurent-Prache (6th).

Victor Hugo by Auguste Rodin in the Jardin des Poètes, Bois de Boulogne (16th).

Square du Temple (3rd);
opposite: private garden
belonging to a religious order
(14th).

La Défense, Paris's skyscraper district, sprang up in the 1960s in order to provide corporate office space unavailable inside the city limits. At the far end of the enormous esplanade is the Grande Arche (1989). It not only echoes but stands in line with Paris's other arches – the Arc du Carrousel and the Arc de Triomphe.

The Stade de France, in the nearby suburb of Saint-Denis, went up in record time in order to host the 1998 FIFA World Cup Final. As everyone recalls, France won that championship. With its seating capacity of over 80,000, the stadium serves not only for major sports events, but for concerts and shows.

Versailles started out as a princely hunting lodge well before it figured in the dreams of young Louis XIV. The king was twenty-three when construction began. To keep construction rolling, he ordered new marble and stone quarries to be opened and had new silk mills, tapestry, porcelain and mirror factories set up. Despite a workforce of forty thousand laborers, the Sun King's soldiers were sometimes sent in as reinforcements to speed production. Construction of the chateau itself was carried out by architect Le Vau, while the gardens were the responsibility of Le Nôtre. After Le Vau's death, Jules Hardouin-Mansart built the Hall of Mirrors and the chapel. Construction lasted nearly fifty years, during practically the entire reign of Louis XIV. The finest chateau in the world was not only a royal residence, but the nation's political center, and the court's headquarters.

One third of Versailles' construction budget reportedly went to conveying water to a naturally dry site. The king's gardens, pools, and fountains required vast quantities of water. Aqueducts, canals, and channels totaling dozens of kilometers were laid out to direct water to where it was needed.

Photos © Jacques Lebar
www.jacqueslebar.com

Édition : Laurence Solnais
Direction artistique : Isabelle Chemin

Avec la collaboration de Lilith Cowan

Achevé d'imprimer en U.E. en mai 2013
ISBN : 978-2-84096-596-1
Dépôt légal : mai 2010